Cali Chloe,
Best Wishes!
xx

This book is dedicated to my angel Stella. Always follow your dreams my darling.

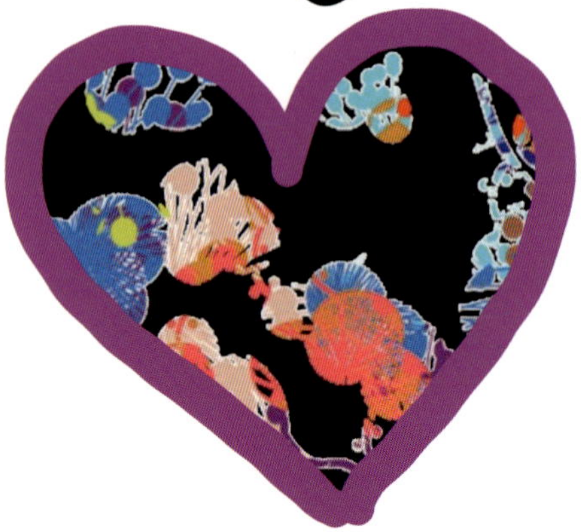

THIS BOOK BELONGS TO:

WITH LOVE FROM:

F is for Fashion
published in 2019 by
PS Publishing
313 NE 3rd Street
Delray Beach, FL, 33444
www.pspublishing.co
www.fisforfashionbook.com

Library of Congress Control Number: 2019948355

ISBN 978-1-7334268-1-7

Illustrated digitally
Designed by Amanda Perna & Solomon Strul

Printed in China
1 2 3 4 5 6 7 8 9 10

This book is a special edition created exclusively for Neiman Marcus.

PS Publishing books are available at special discounts when purchased in quantity for premiums and promotions as well as fundraising or educational use. Special editions can also be created to specification. For details, contact info@pspublishing.co.

PUBLISHING

F is for Fashion

Written By Amanda Perra + Solomon Strul
Illustrated By: Amanda Perra

PS PUBLISHING

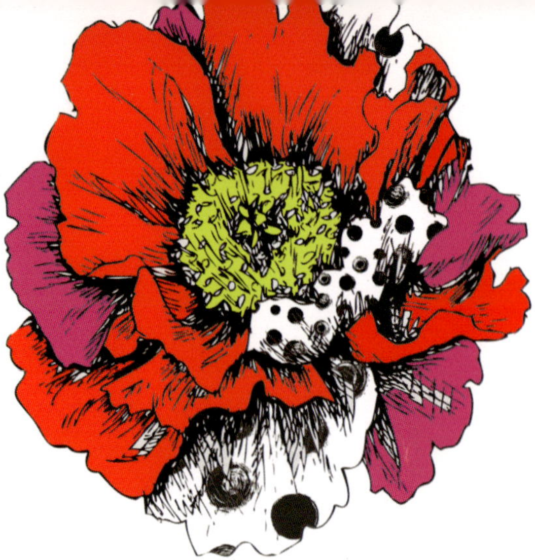

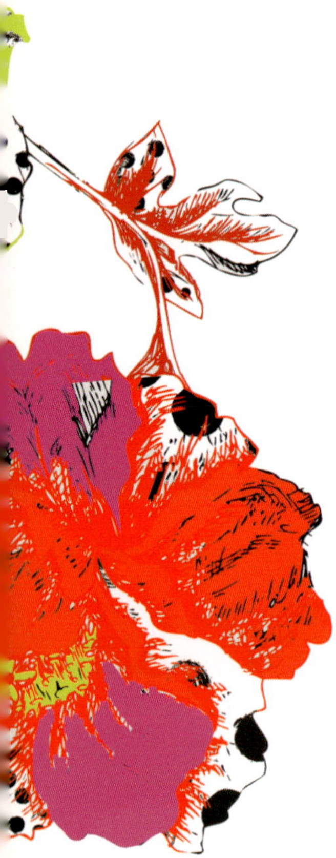

Aa

is for A-line (dress)

a is for a-line (dress)

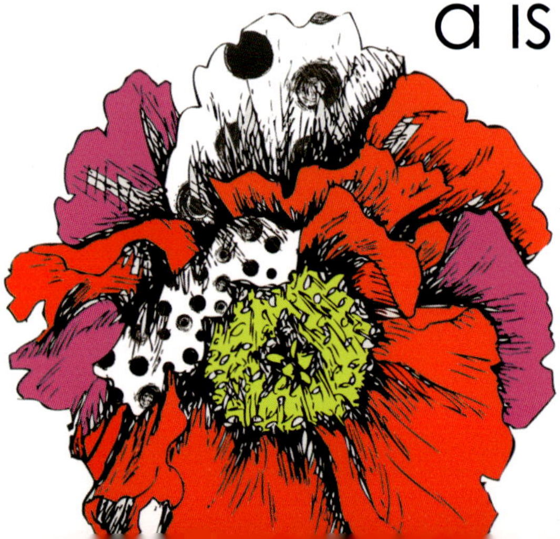

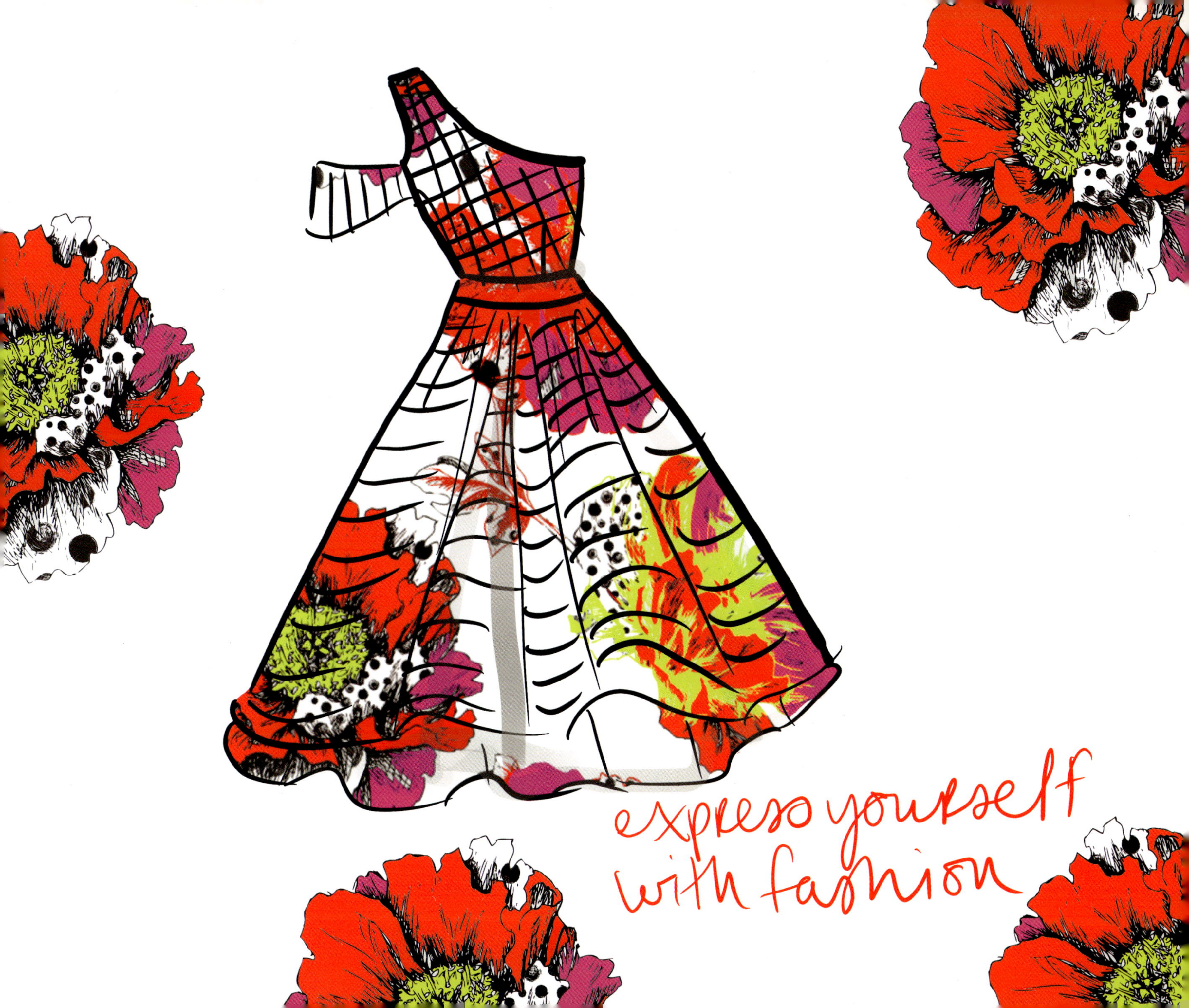
express yourself
with fashion

Bb

is for bathingsuit

b is for bathing suit

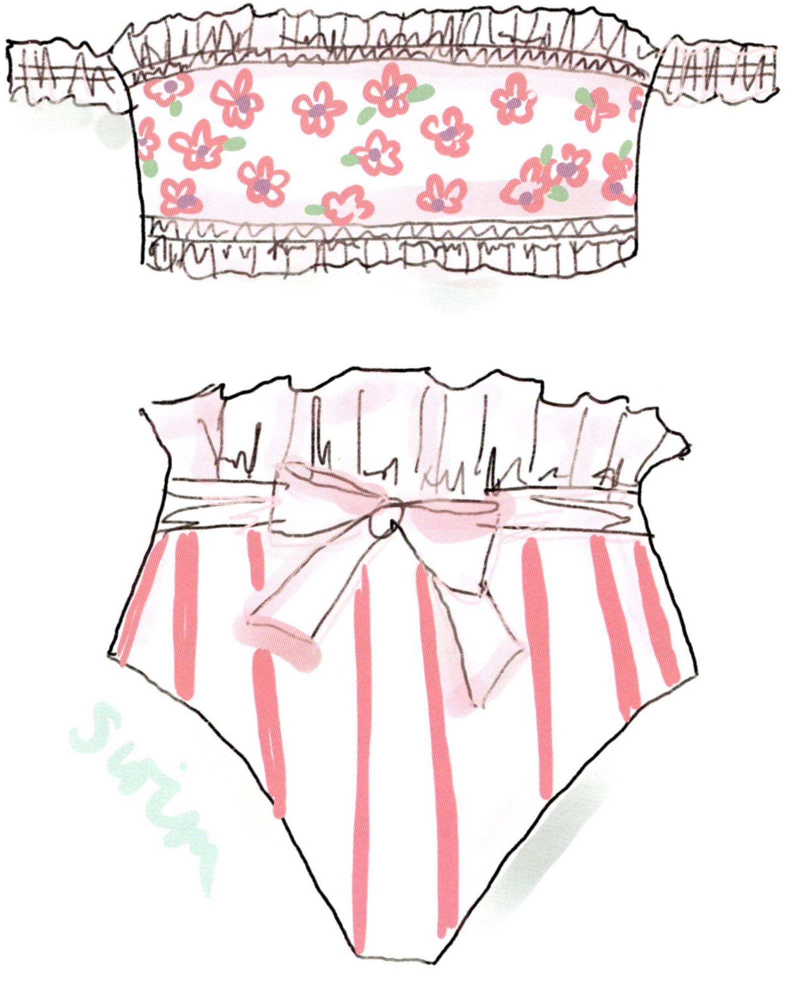
swim

Cc

is for coat

c is for coat

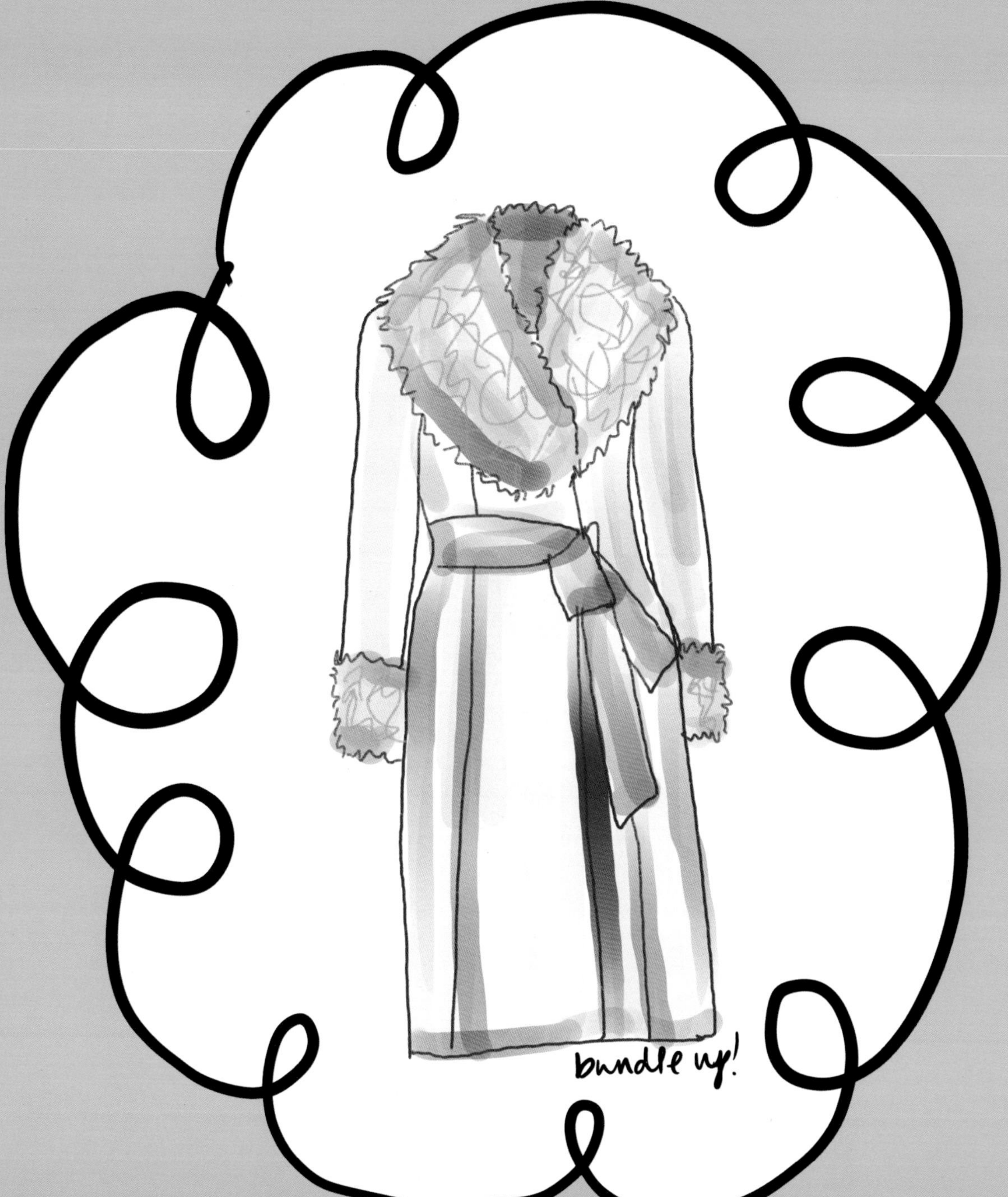
bundle up!

Dd

is for dress

d is for dress

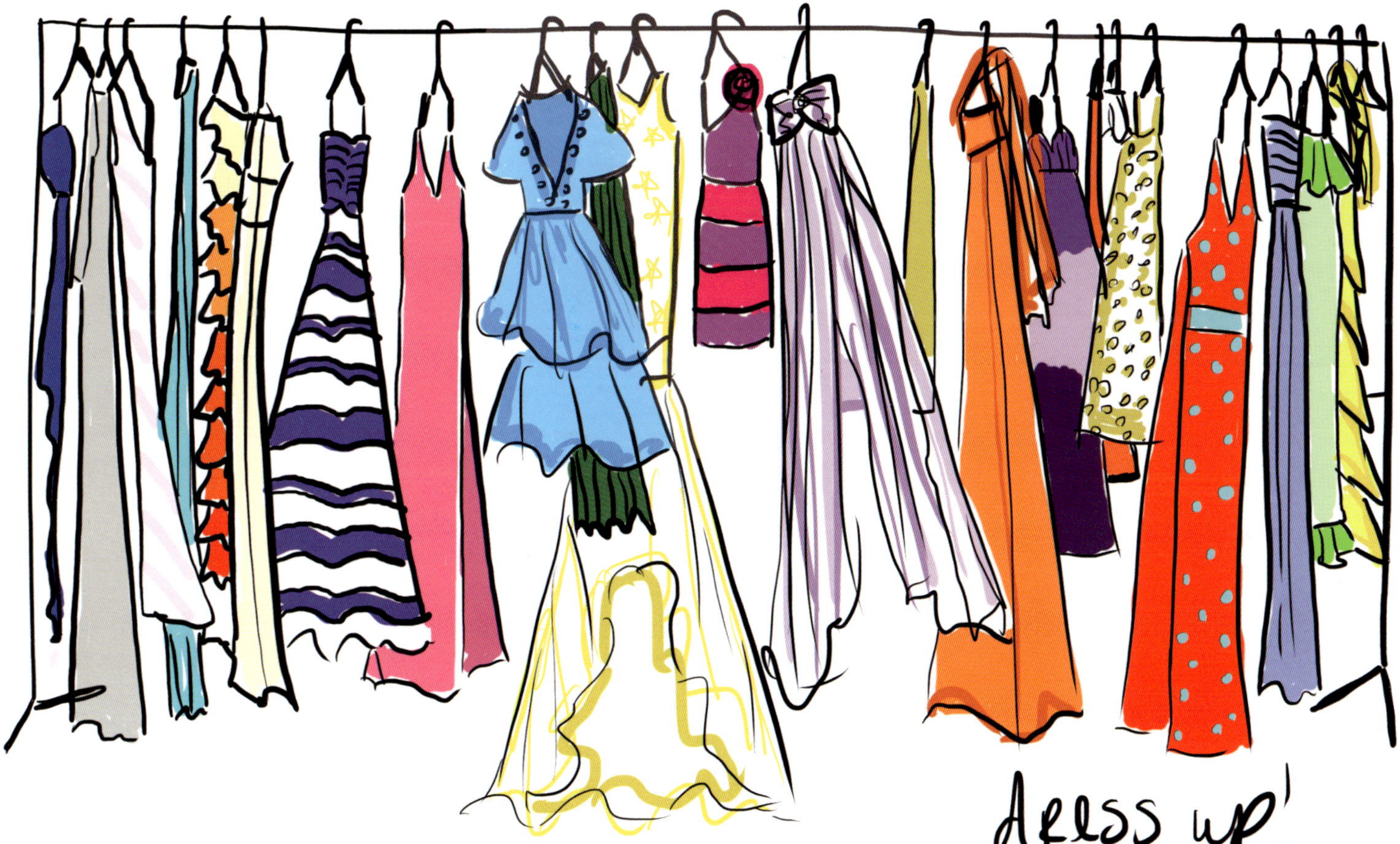

dress up!

Ee

is for earring

e is for earring

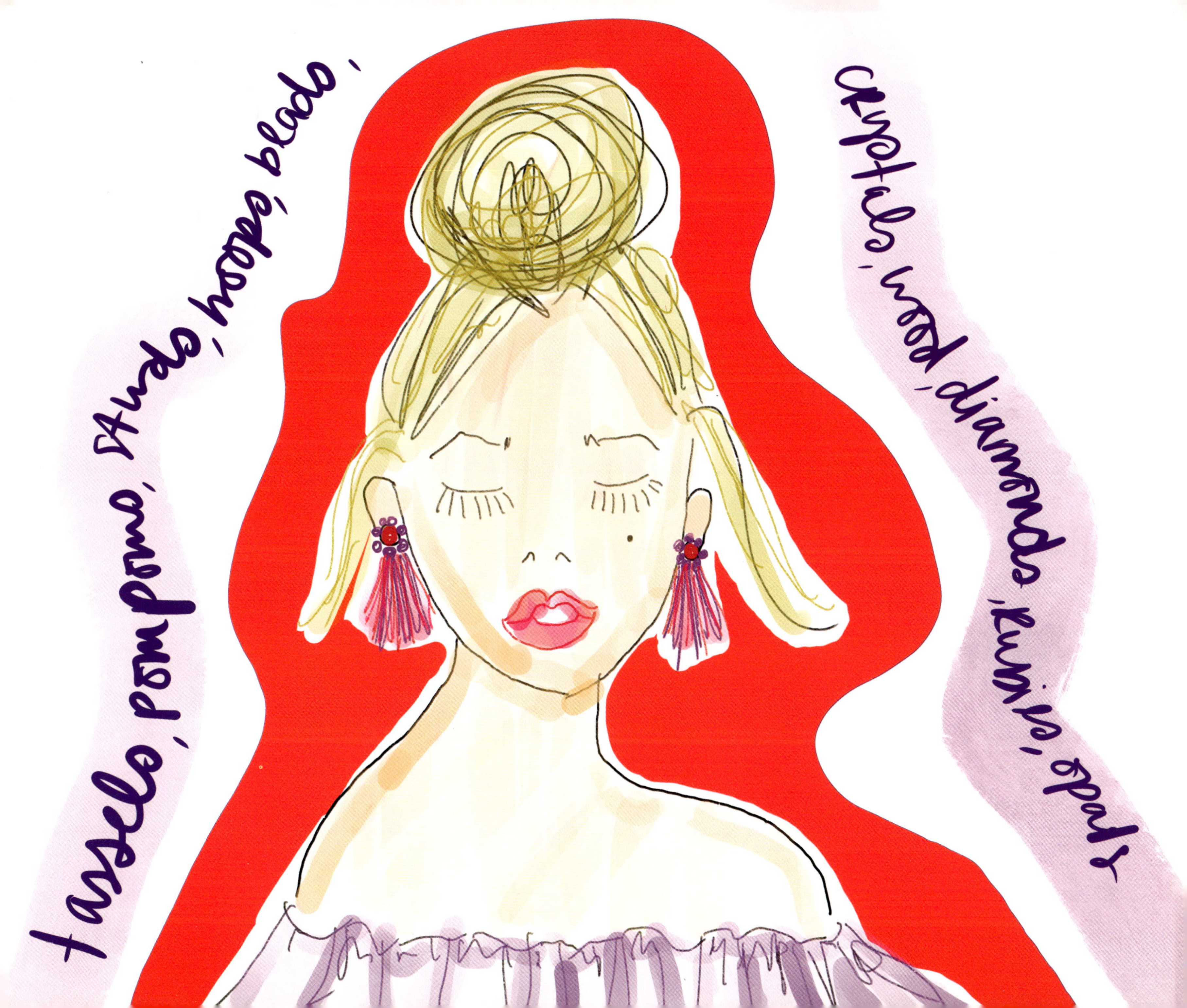
tassels, pompoms, studs, hoops, beads,
crystals, wool, diamonds, rubies, opals

Ff

is for fashion

f is for fashion

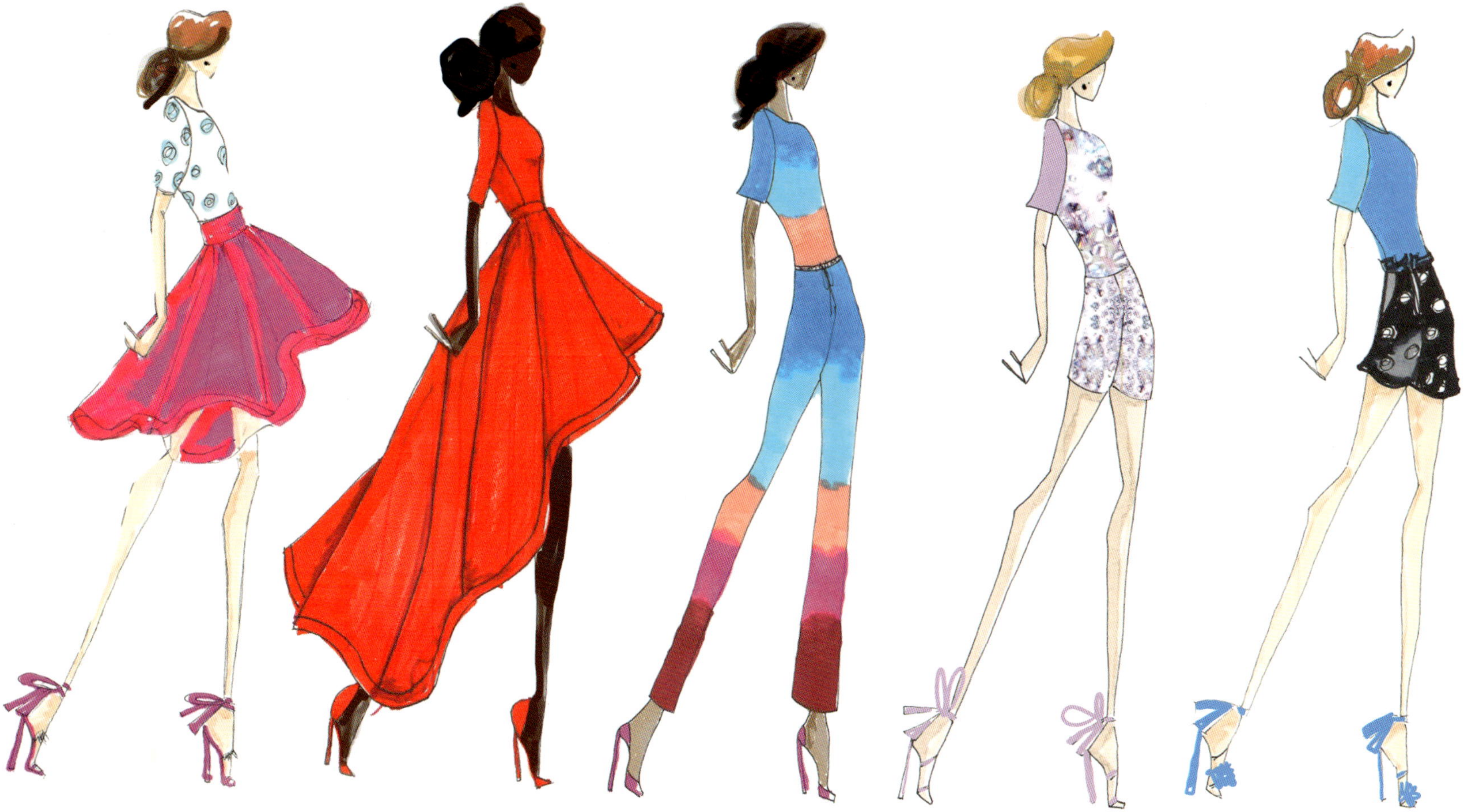

the world is your runway

Gg

is for glasses

g is for glasses

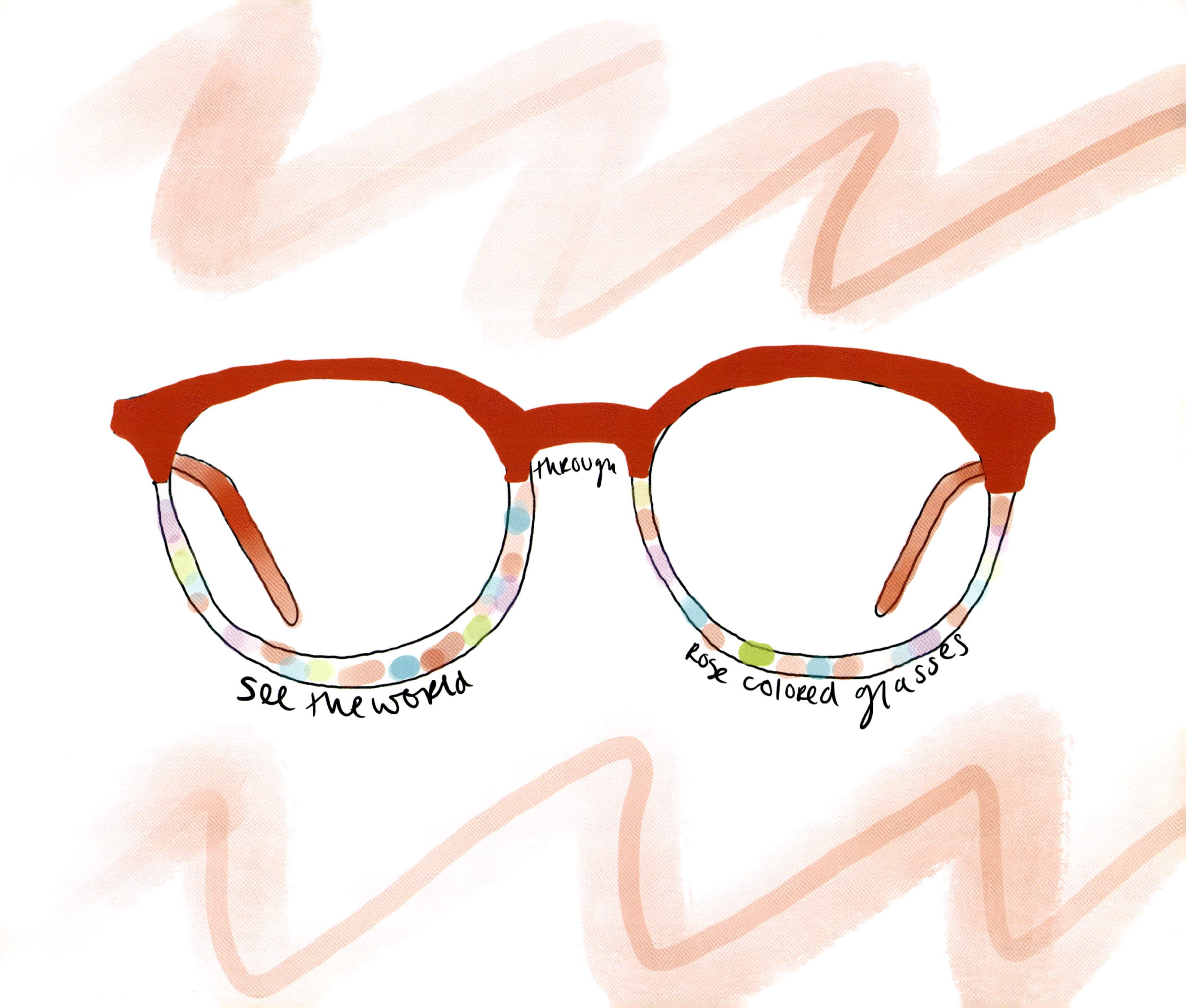
see the world
through
rose colored glasses

Hh

is for hat

h is for hat

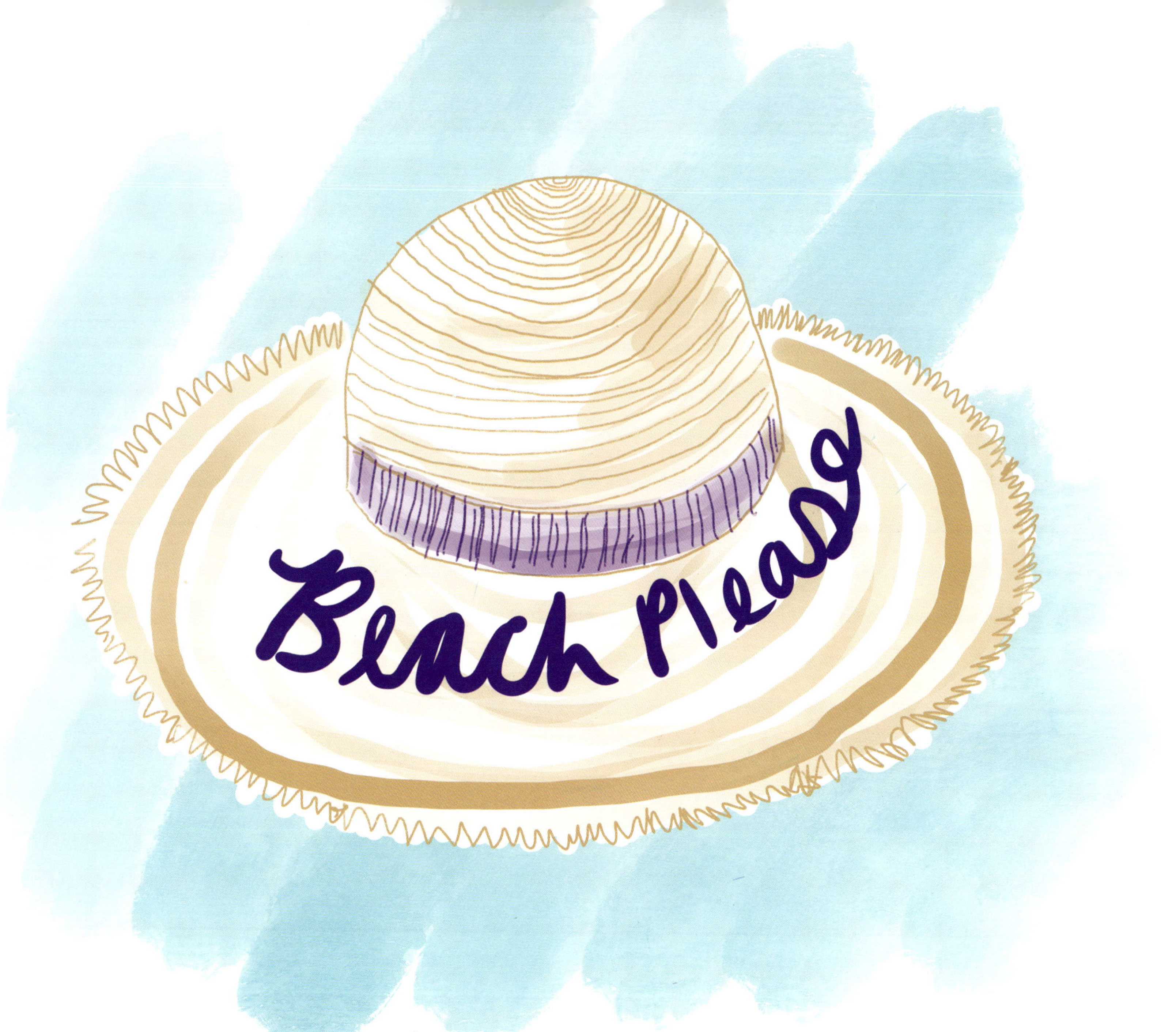
Beach Please

Ii

is for indigo dye

i is for indigo dye

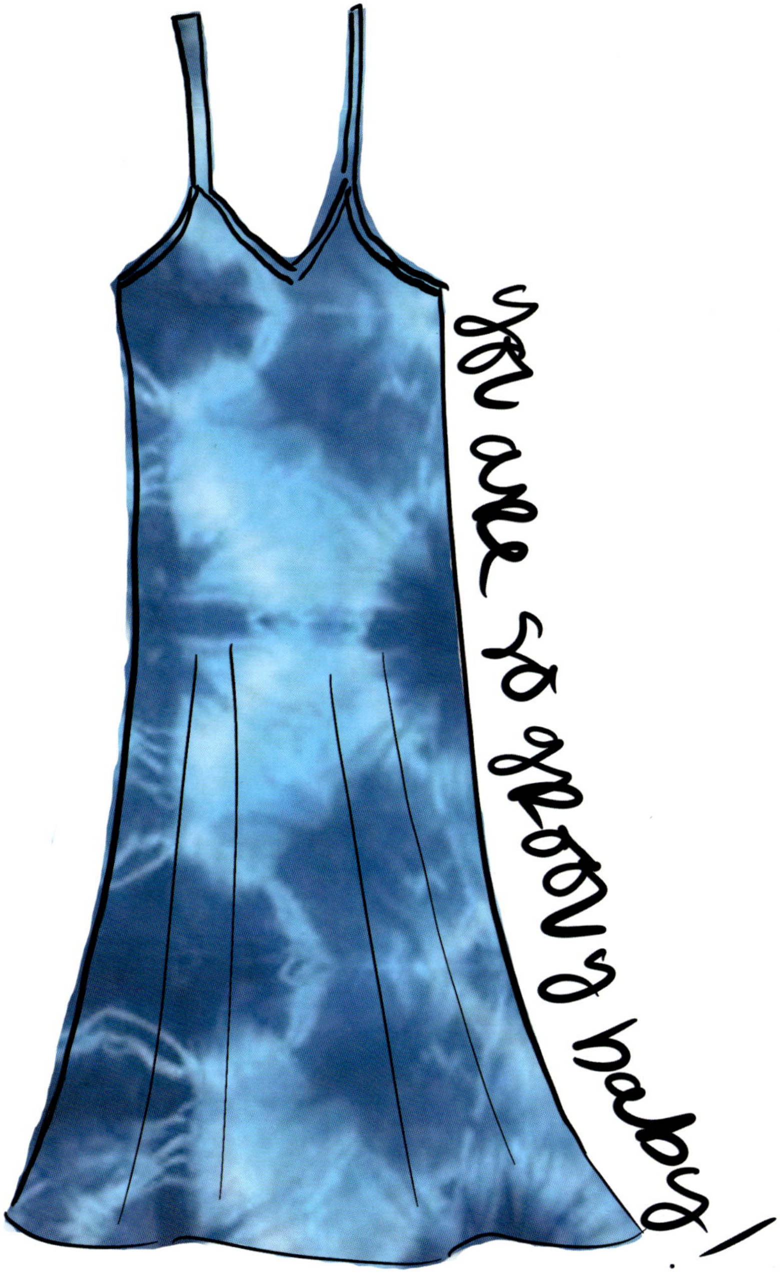
you are so groovy baby!
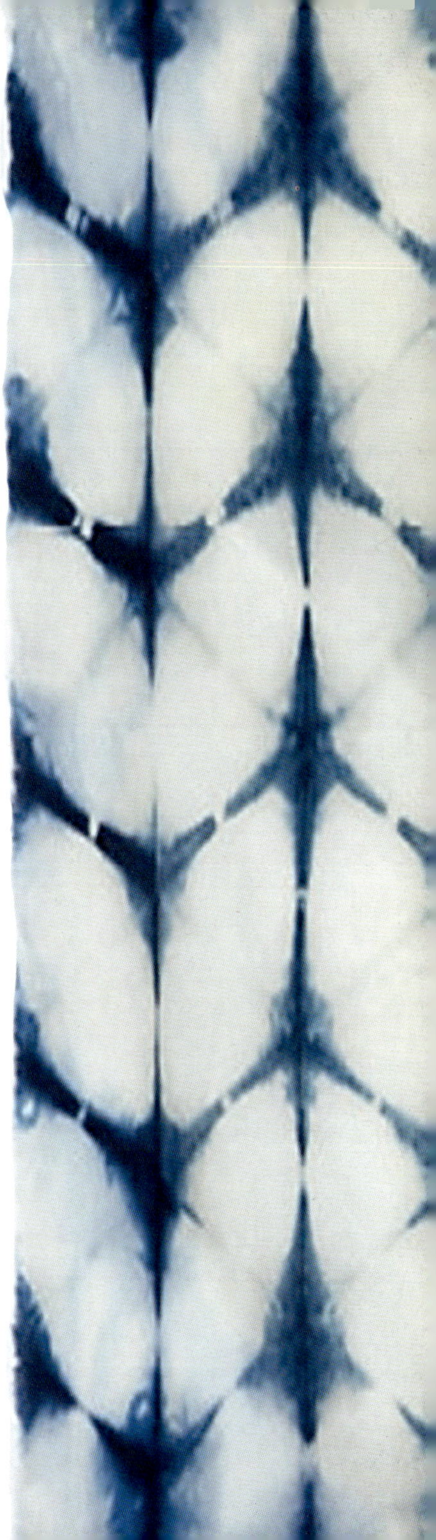

Jj

is for jacket

j is for jacket

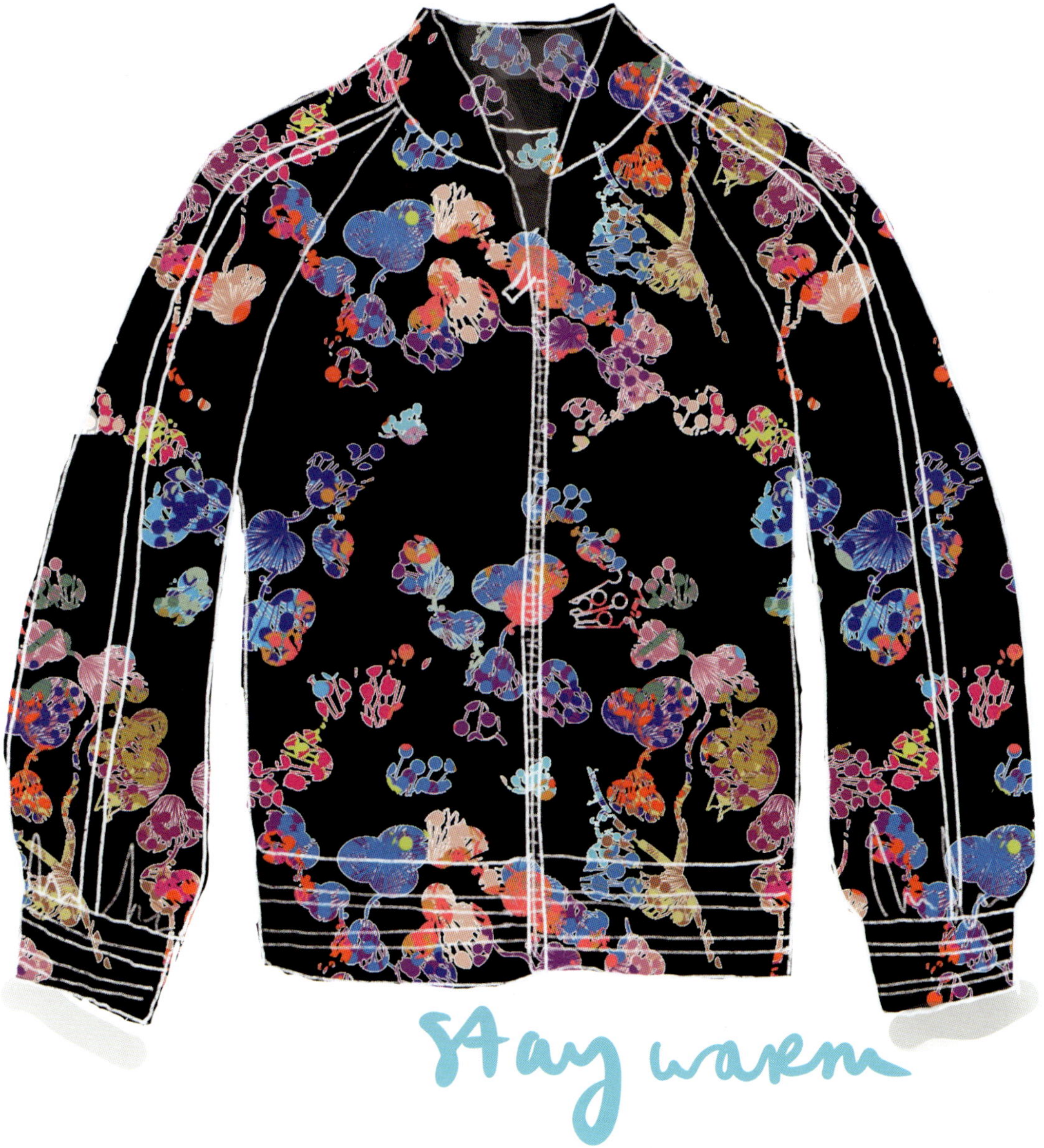
stay warm

Kk

is for kimono

k is for kimono

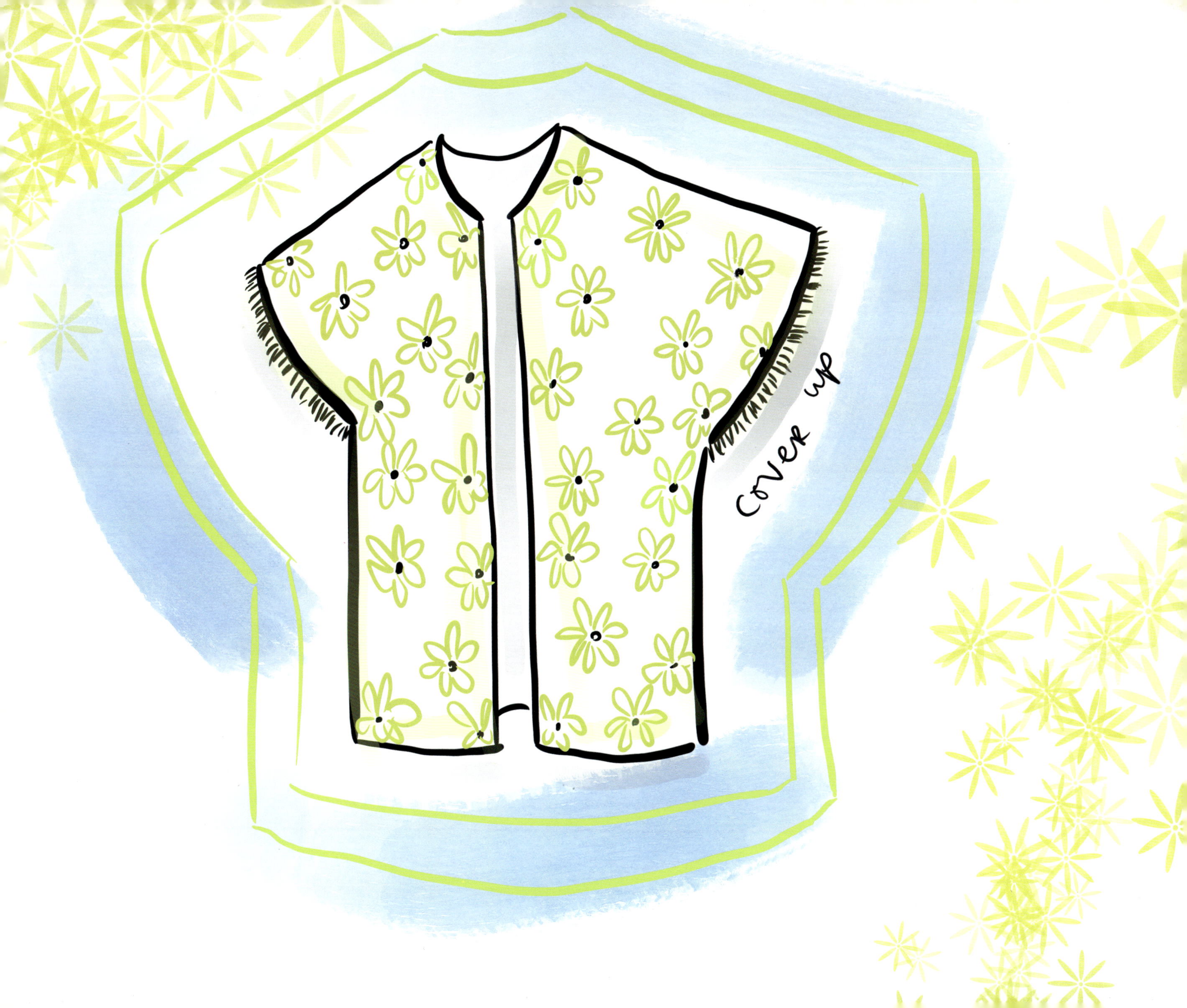
cover up

Ll

is for leggings

l is for leggings

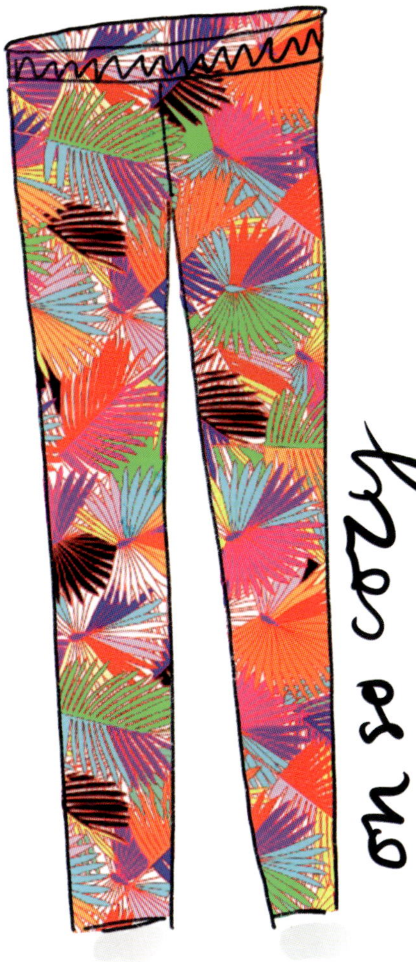
so so cozy

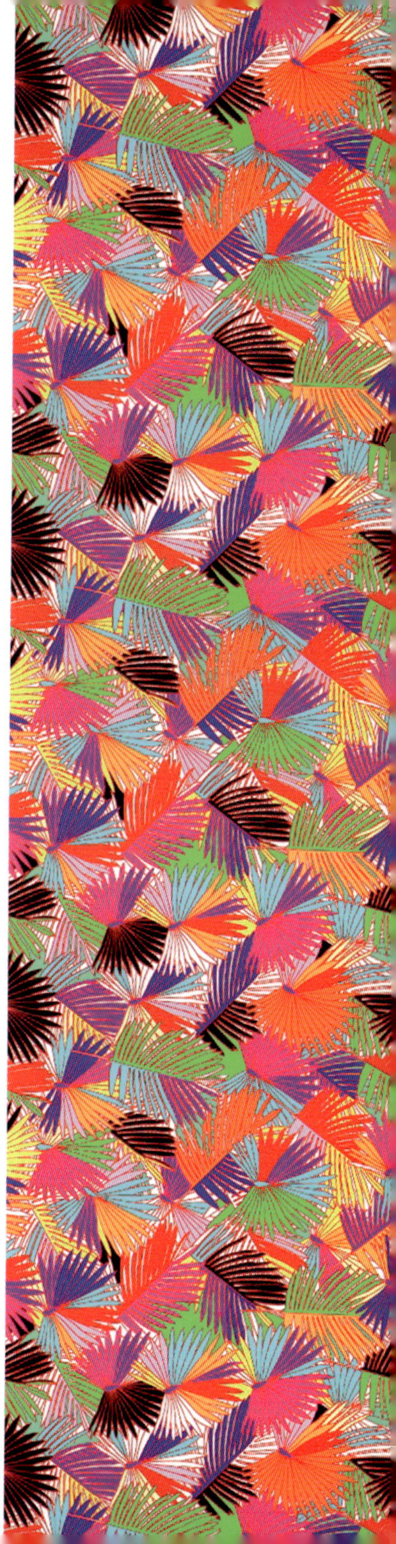

Mm

is for measurement

m is for measurement

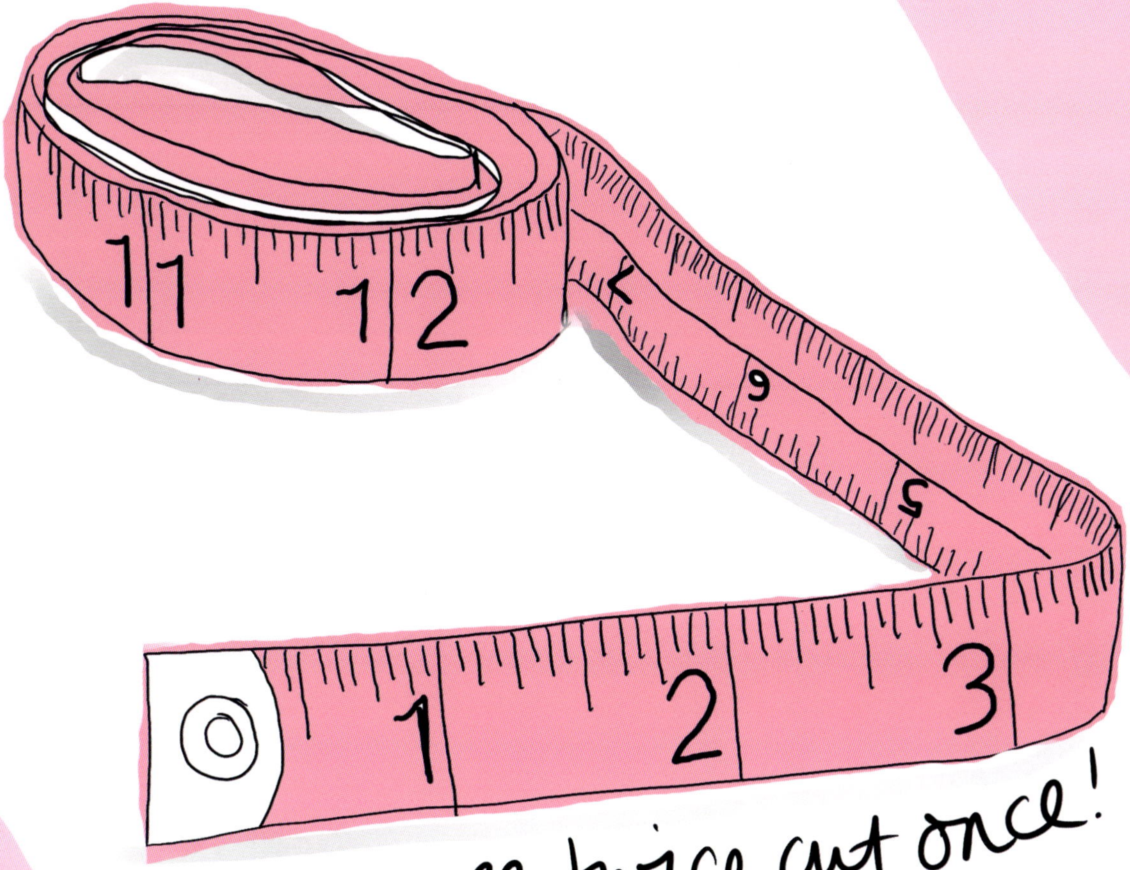

measure twice, cut once!

Nn

is for Neiman Marcus

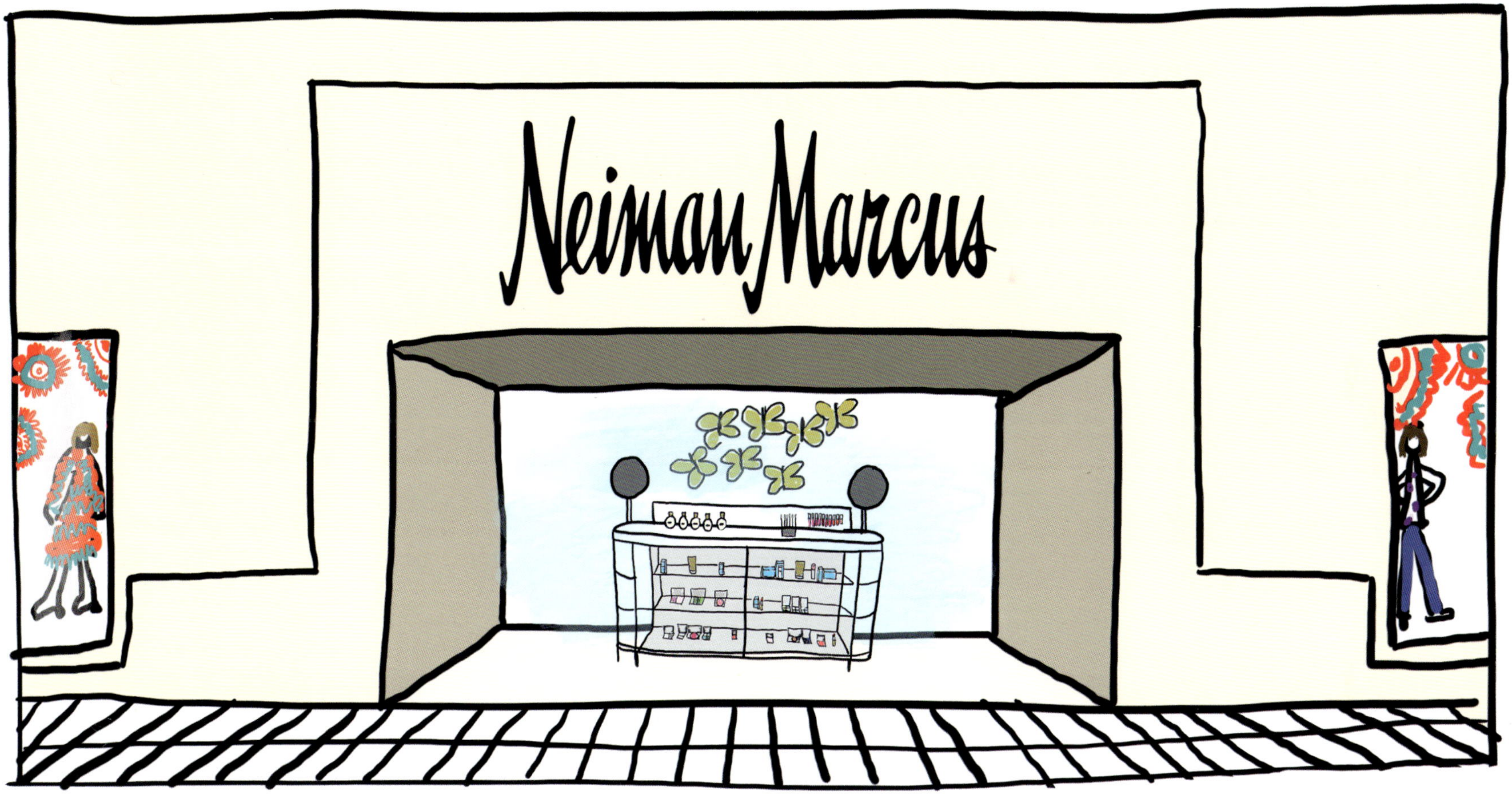
Neiman Marcus

Oo

o is for ombre

o is for ombre

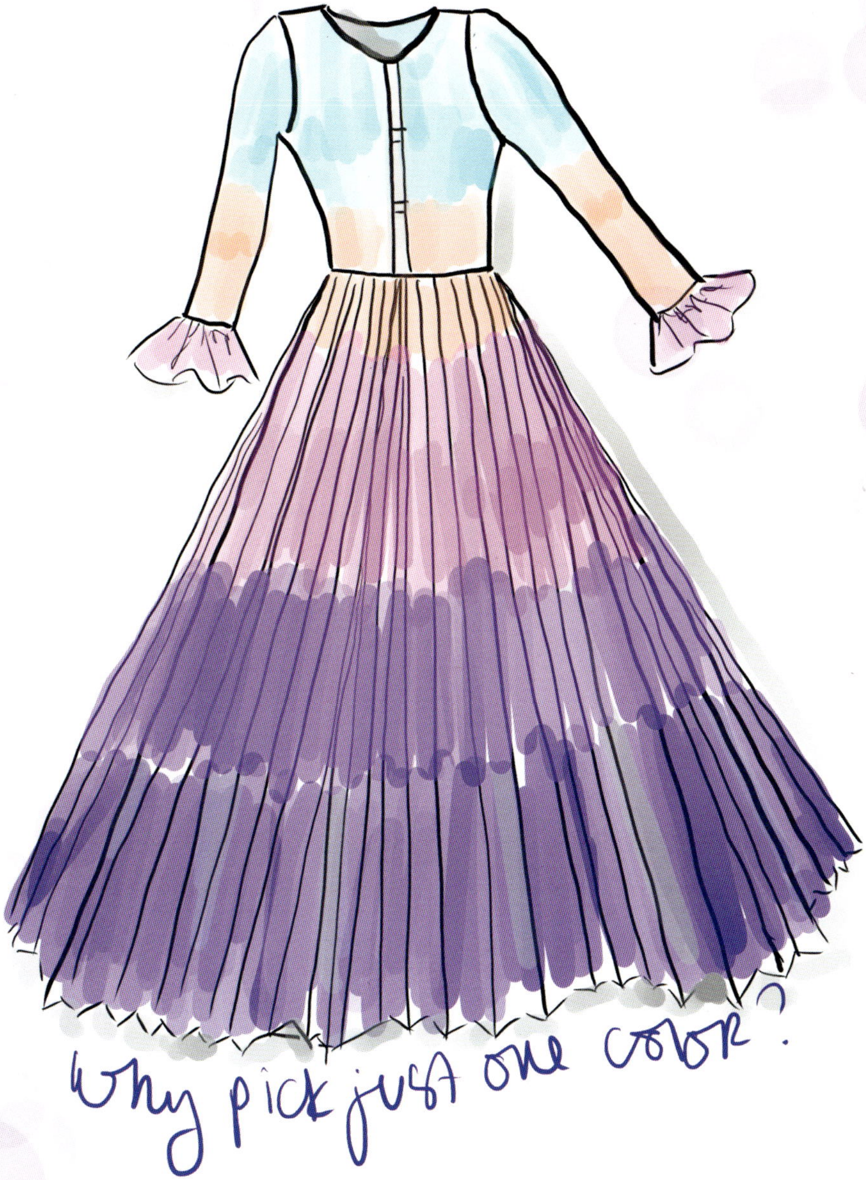

Why pick just one color?

Pp

is for pants

p is for pants

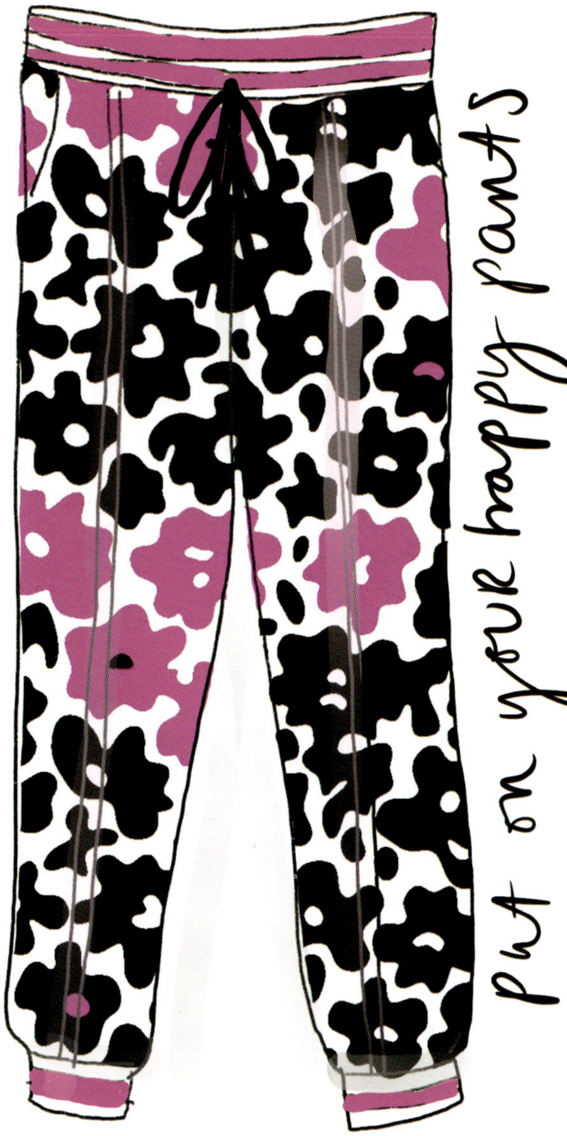
put on your happy pants

Q q

is for quilted

q is for quilted

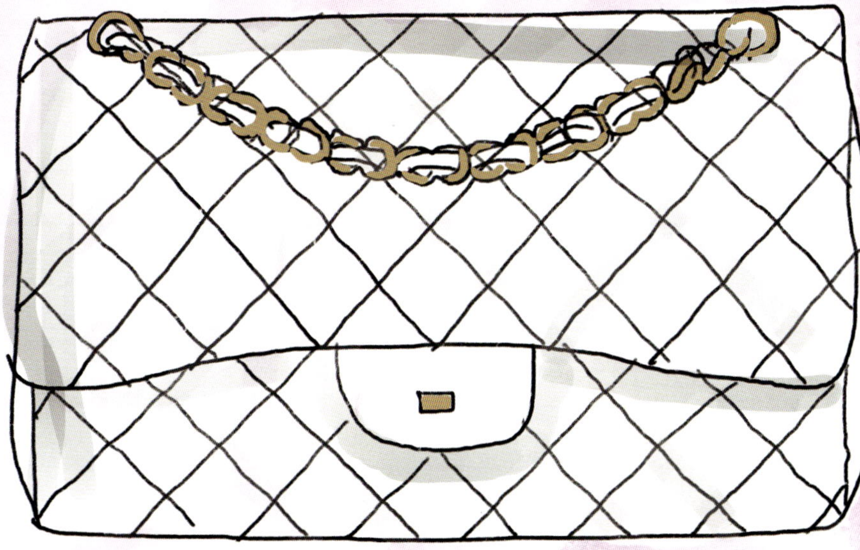

classic + classy

Rr

is for Rainboots

r is for rainboots

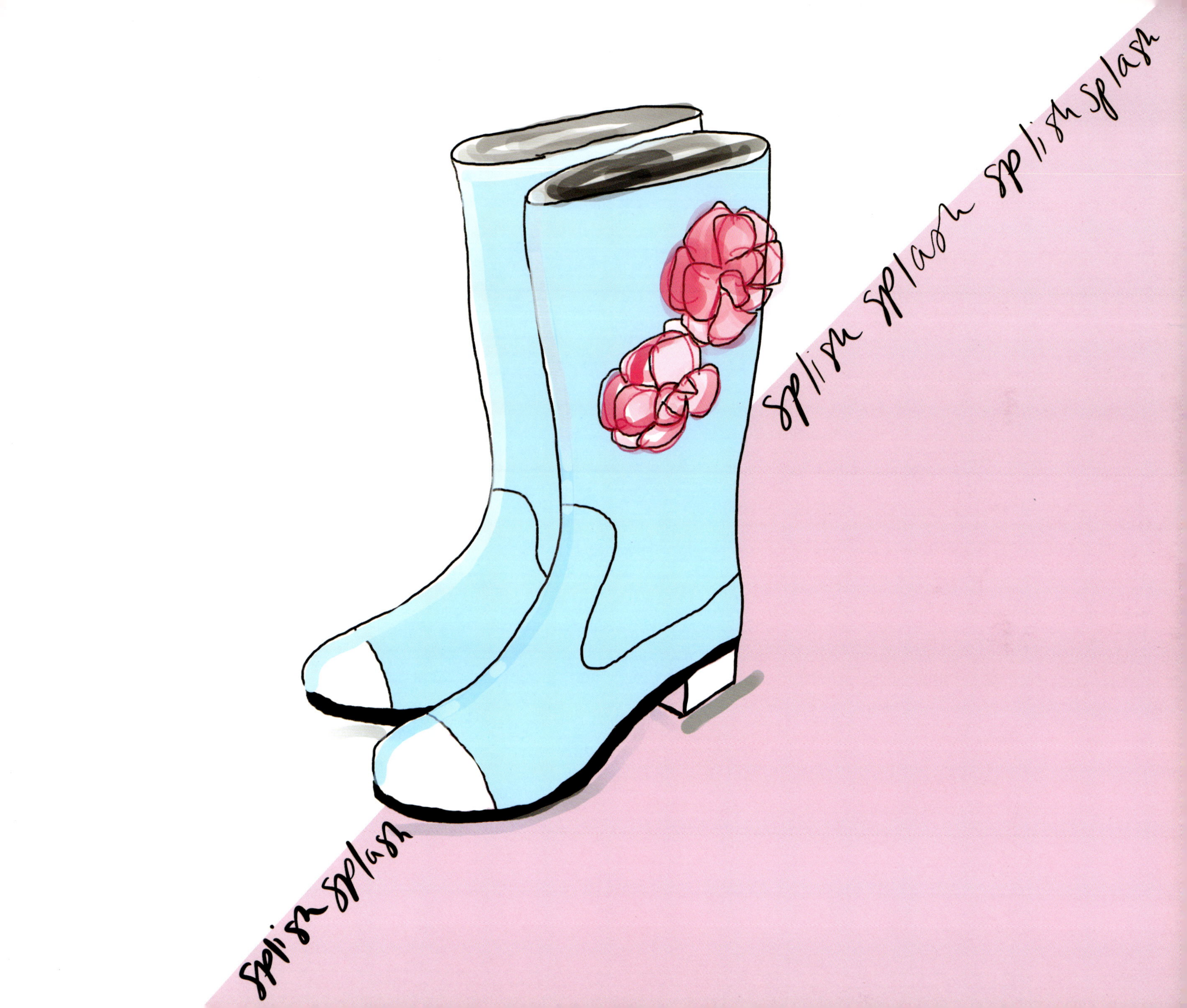
splish splash
splish splash splish splash

Ss

is for shoe

s is for shoe

Heels, platform, flat, wedge, boots, clogs,
pumps, sandals, mules, pumps, booties,
pointy, round toe, metal
printed, colorful, tasseled
athletic, running,
over the knee,
slides, patent
leather,
mary jane
dance
tennis, golf,
cleats, high heels
I love them all! more shoes please!

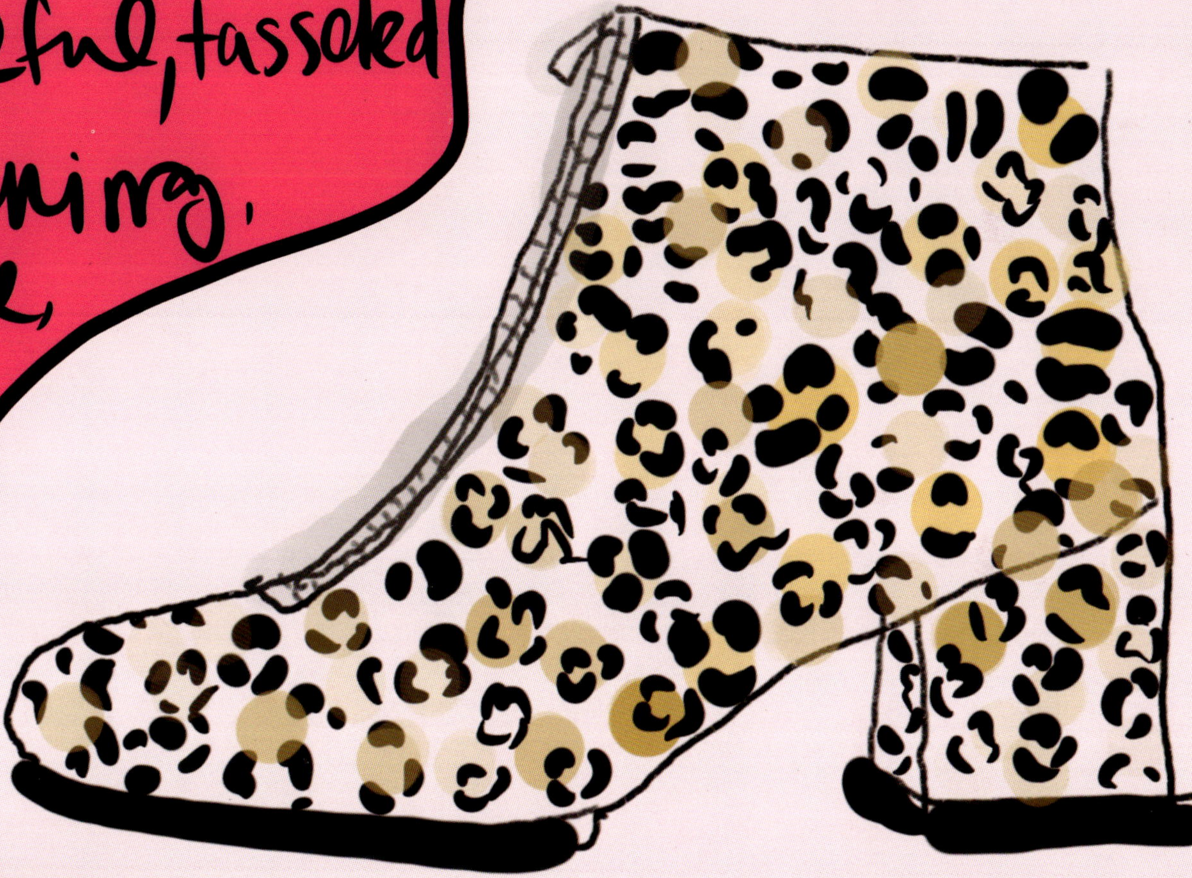

Tt

is for tutu

t is for tutu

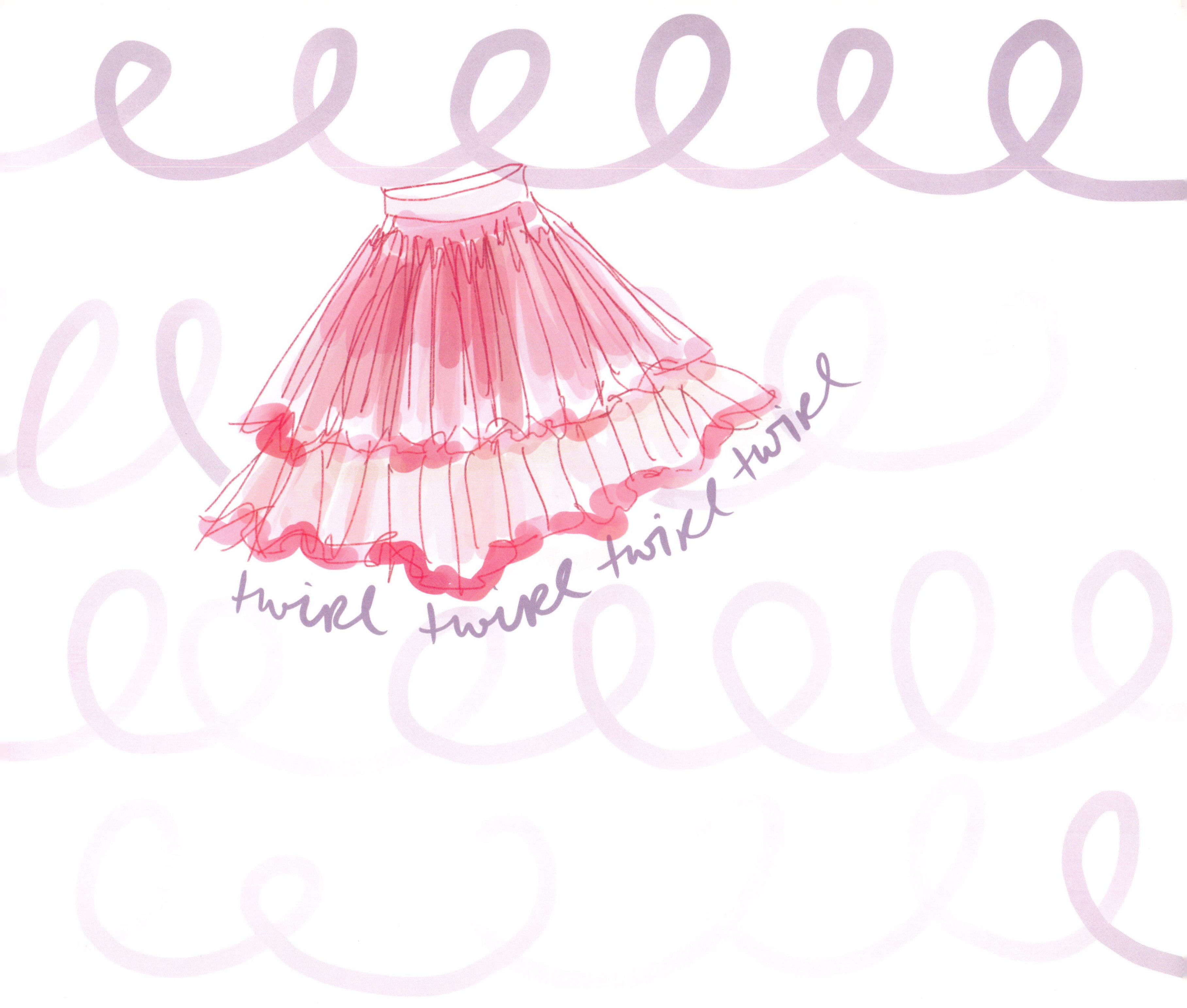
twirl twirl twirl twirl

Uu

is for umbrella

u is for umbrella

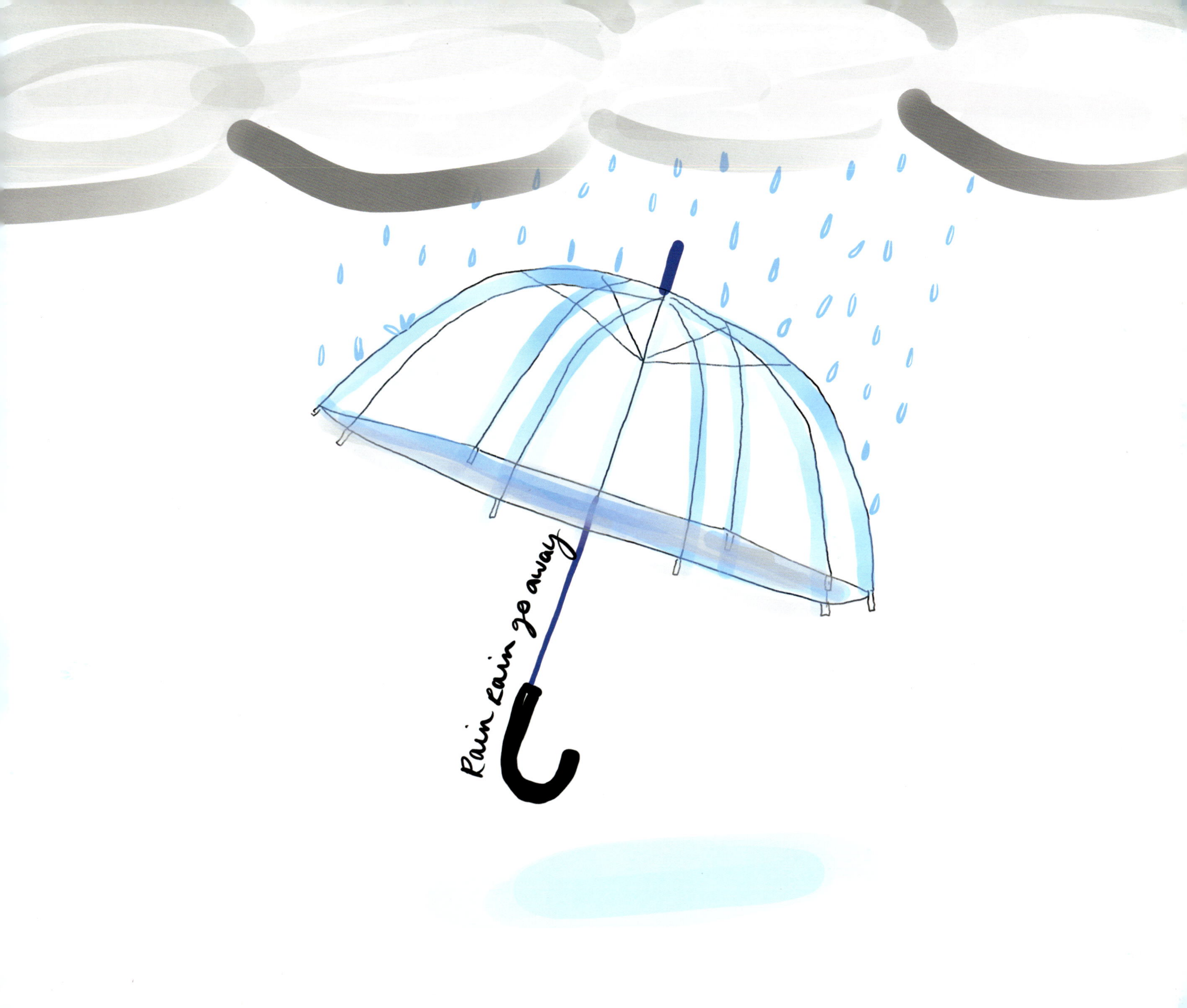
Rain rain go away

Vv

is for vest

v is for vest

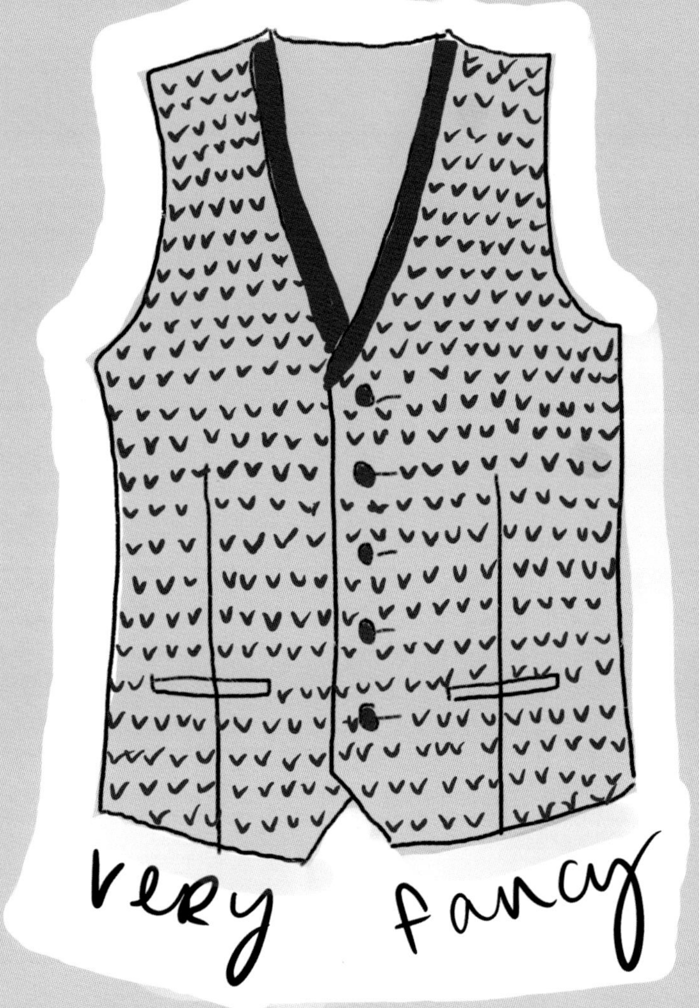
very fancy

Ww

is for watch

w is for watch

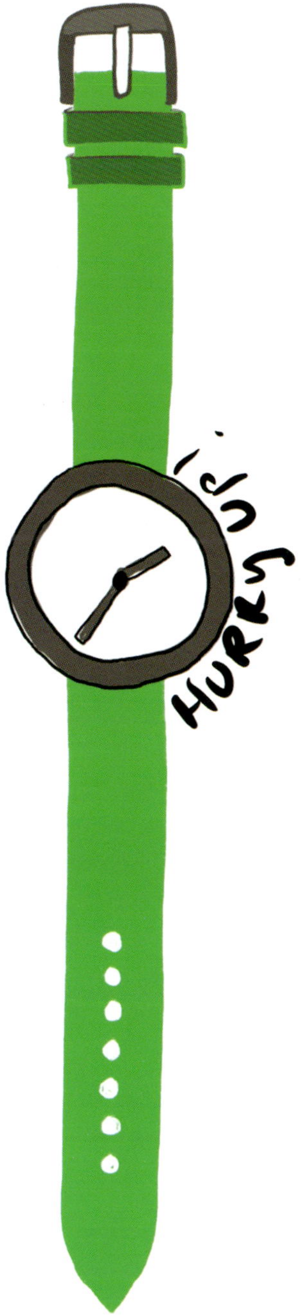
HURRY UP!

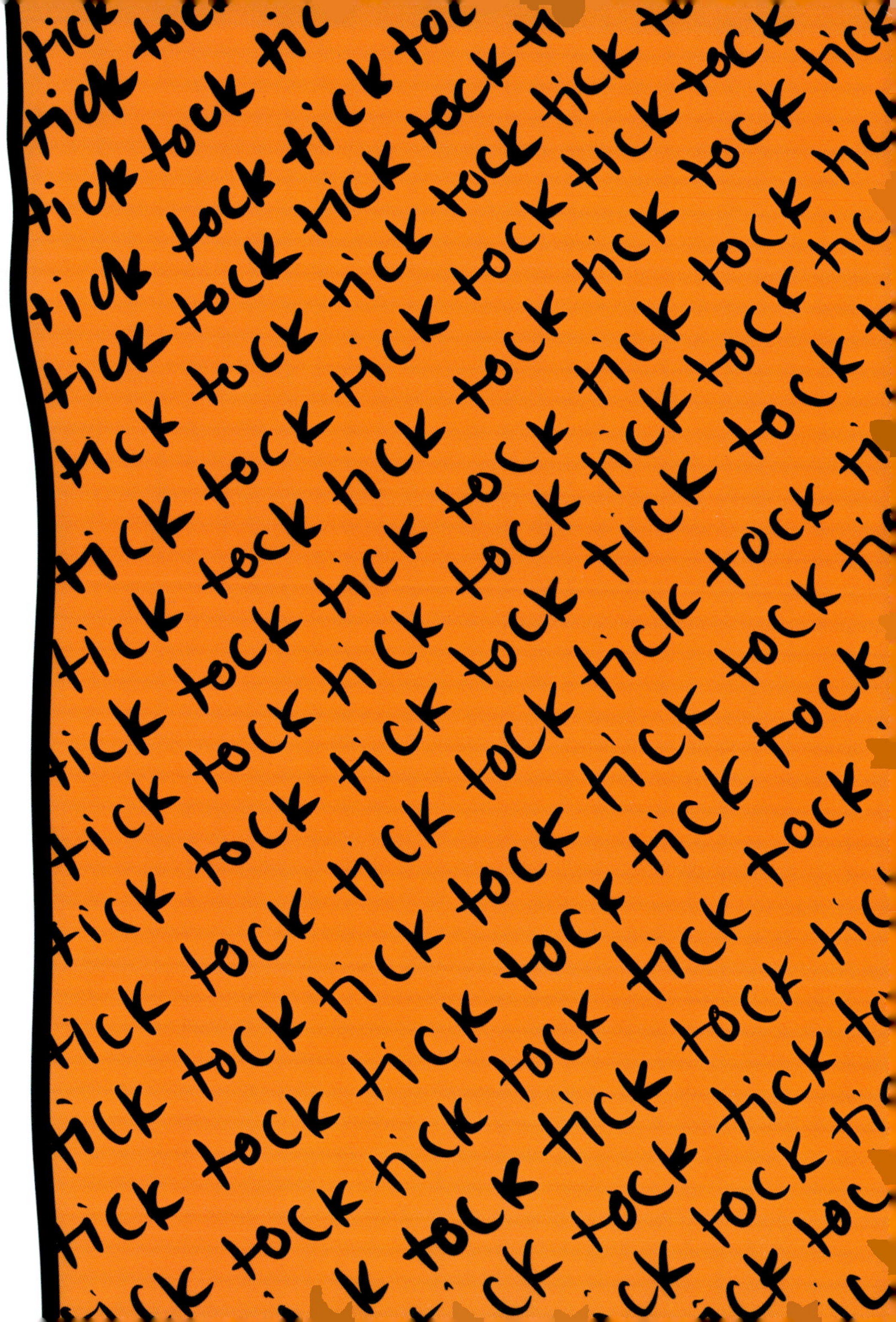
tick tock tick tock tick

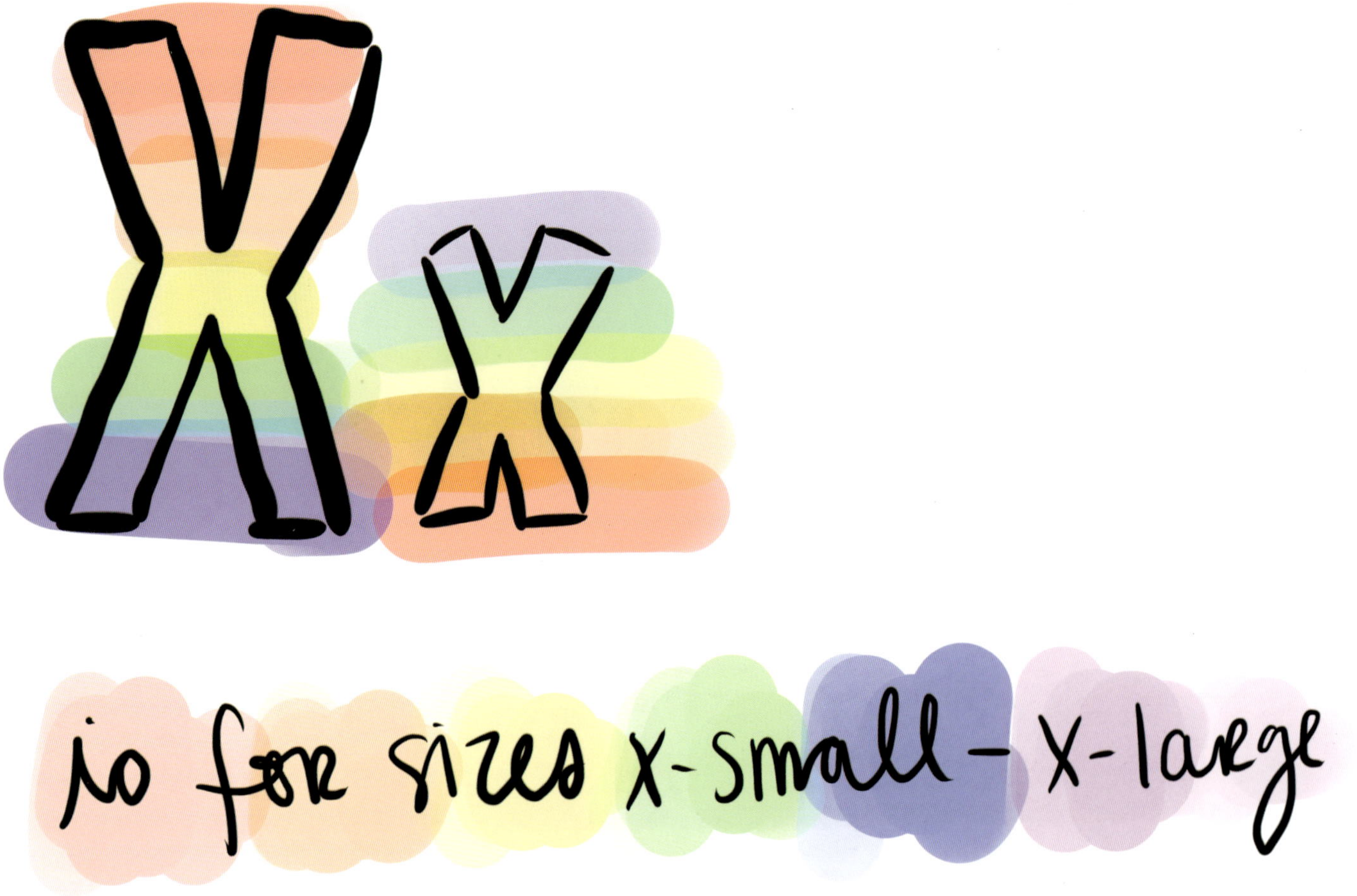

x is for sizes x-small - x-large

Kids size chart

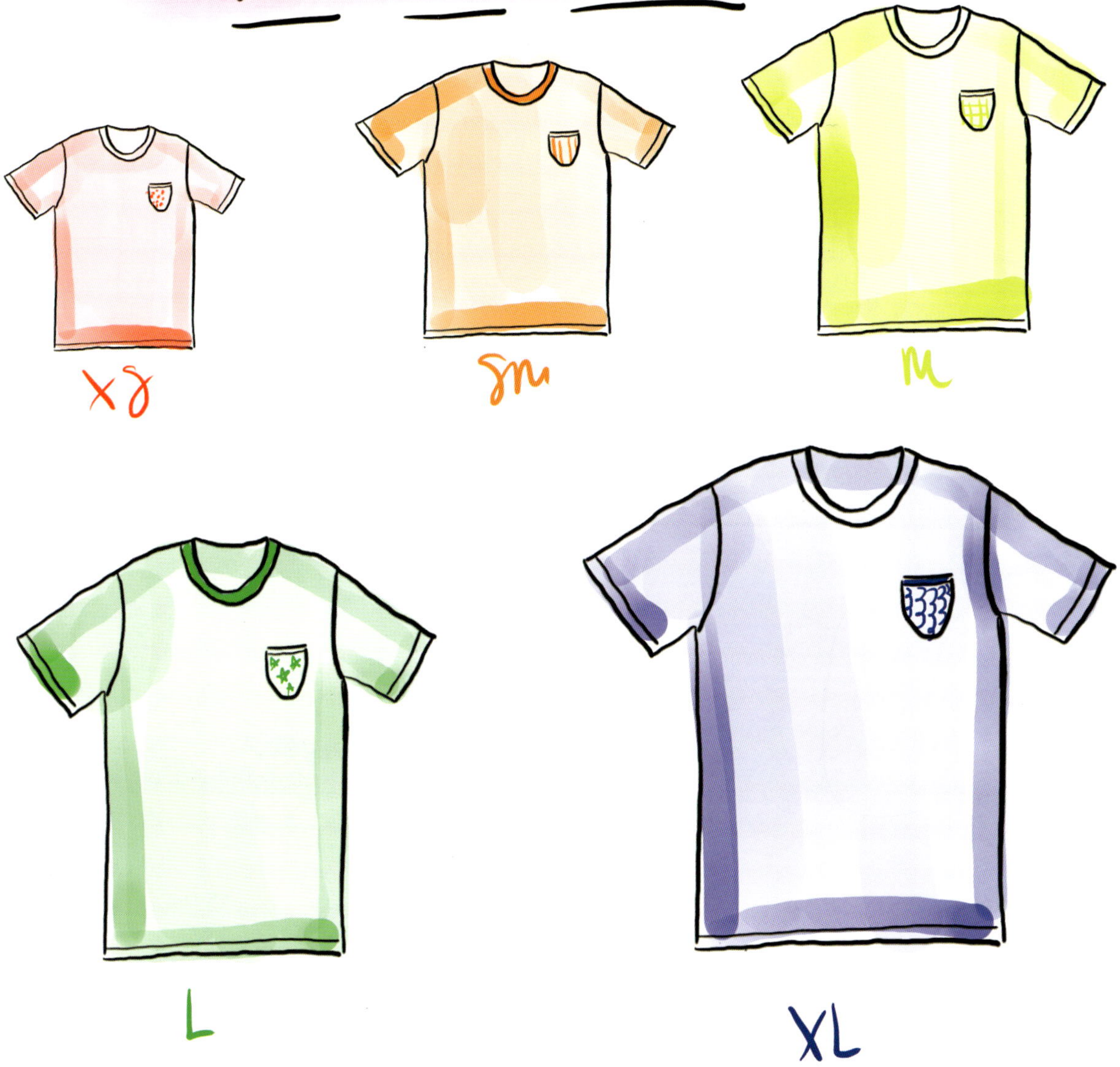

love the size you are! Every size is beautiful!

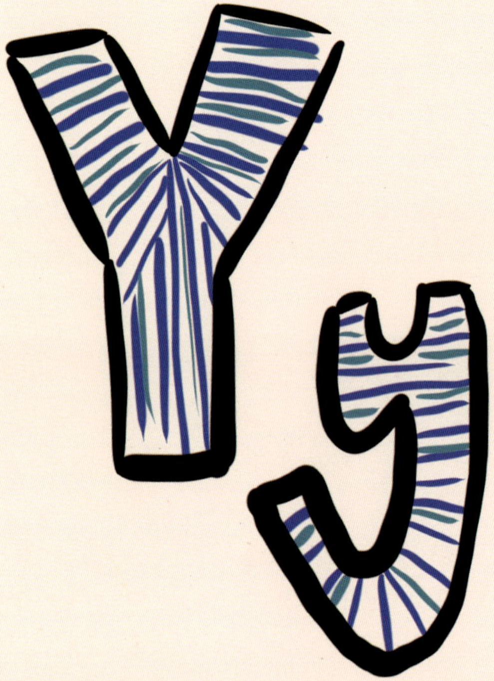

is for yarn dyed

y is for yarn dyed

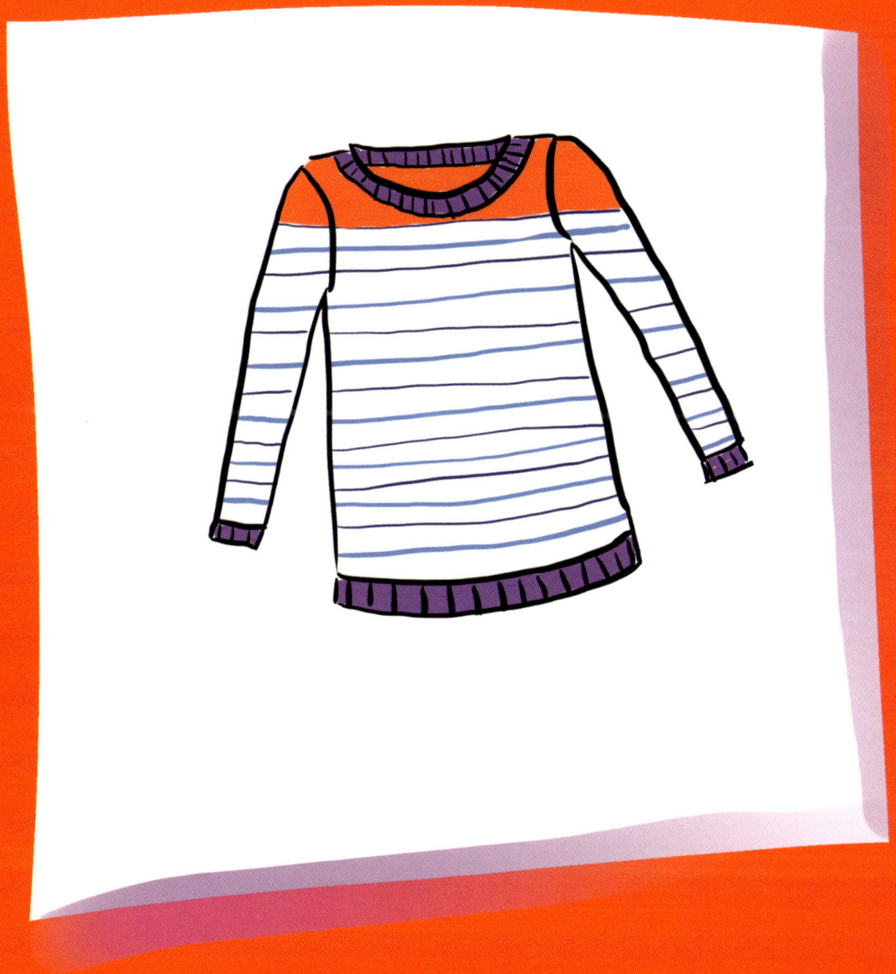

Stripes, oh so many stripes!

Zz

is for zipper

z is for zipper

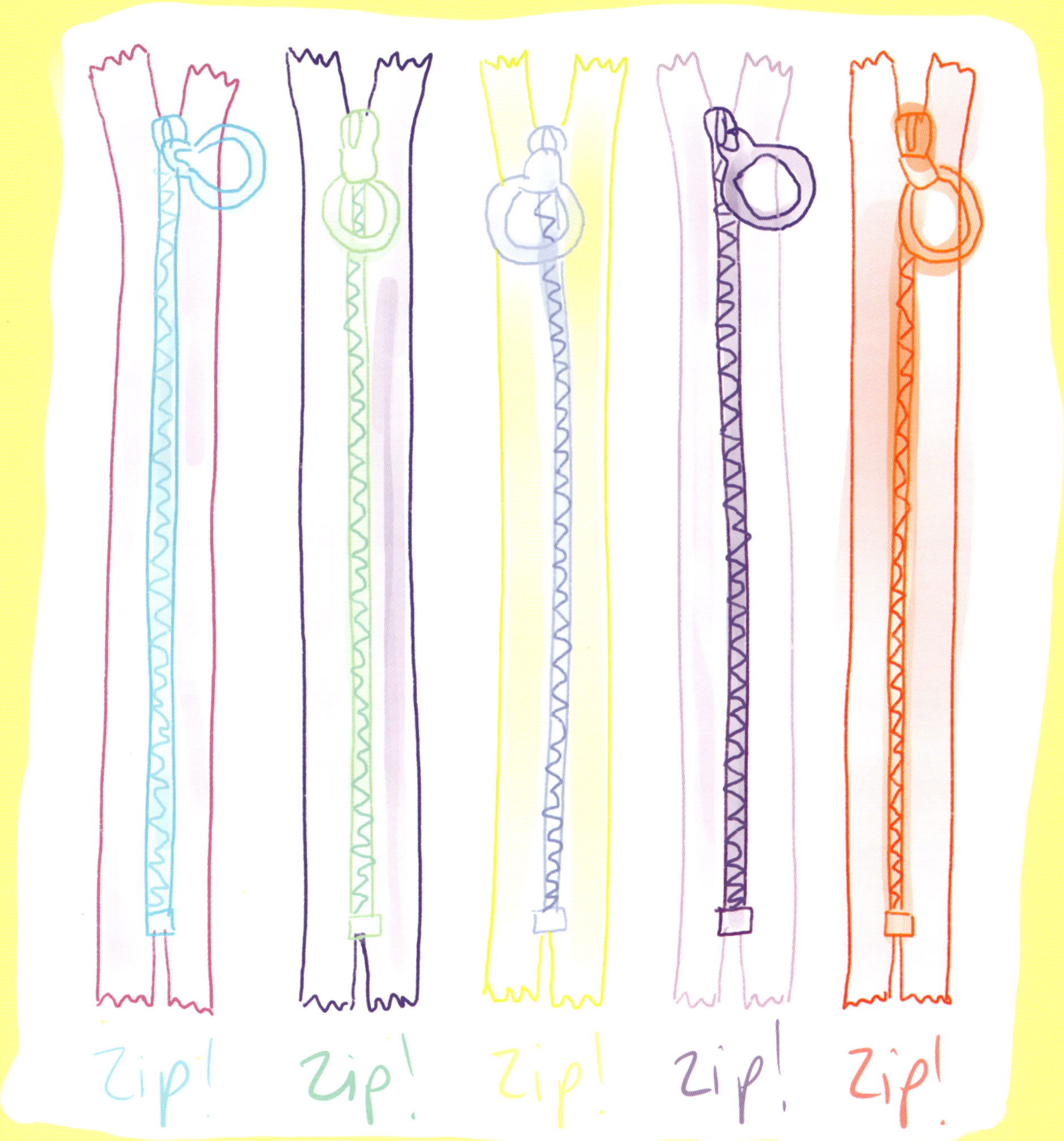
Zip!
Zip!
Zip!
Zip!
Zip!

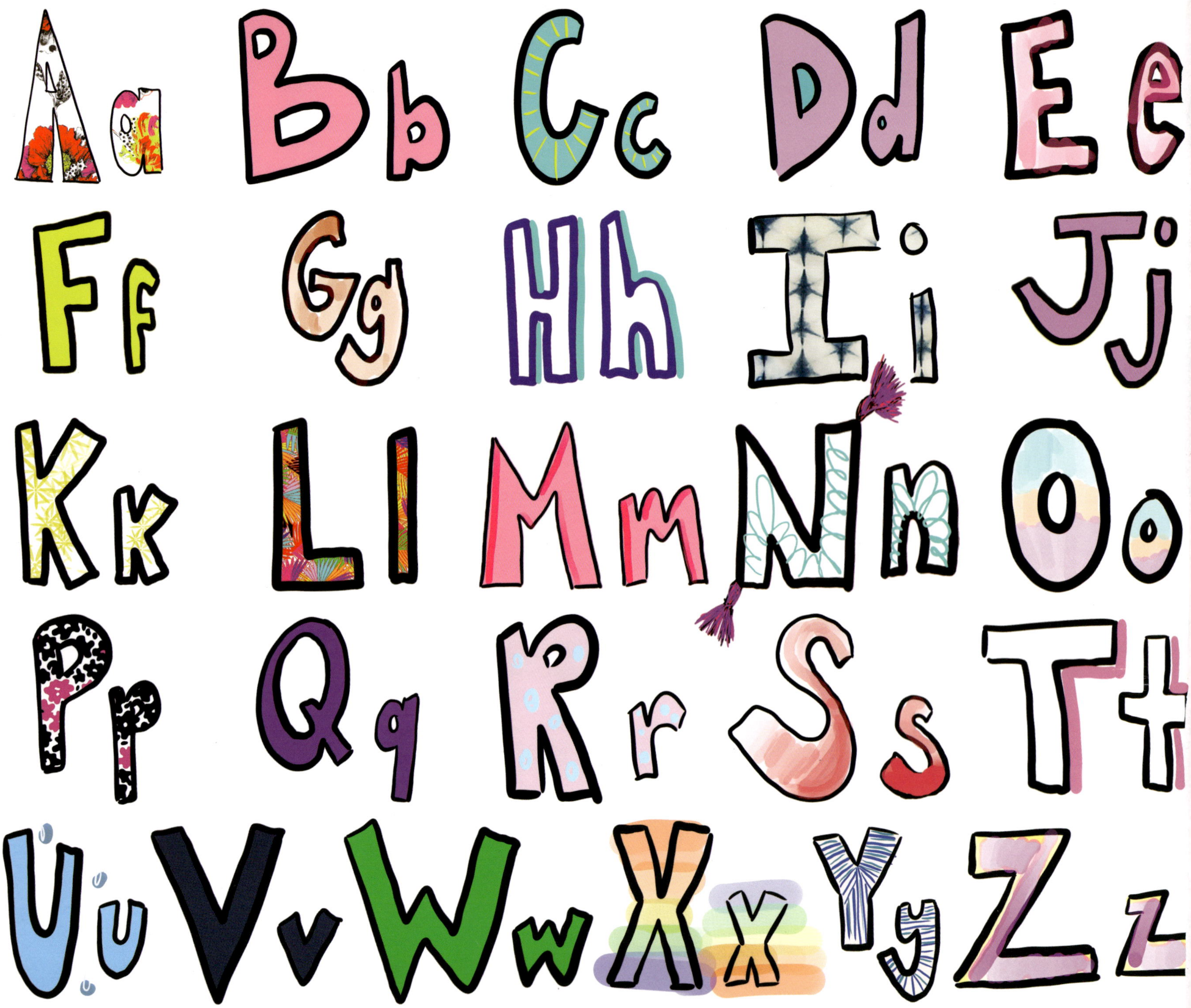
Aa Bb Cc Dd Ee
Ff Gg Hh Ii Jj
Kk Ll Mm Nn Oo
Pp Qq Rr Ss Tt
Uu Vv Ww Xx Yy Zz

Now you know your ABCs, will you come design with me?

The End!

xx

ABOUT THE AUTHORS

AMANDA PERNA & SOLOMON STRUL are a husband and wife team. Amanda is a mom, wife & fashion expert who believes we are stronger together and life is too short not to follow your dreams! Amanda studied Apparel Design at the University of Alabama and FIT and designed for major fashion houses in New York before launching her own brands. She has appeared on internationally renowned TV shows and collaborated with some of the world's most well-known brands and retailers. Solomon is a father, husband & writer who loves to explore the world one word (and sometimes one letter) at a time!

For more information, please visit amandaperna.com or follow @theamandaperna.